Westview Elementary School

BACKYARD WILDLIFE

Rabbits

by Derek Zobel

BELLWETHER MEDIA • MINNEAPOLIS, MN

Note to Librarians, Teachers, and Parents:

Blastoff! Readers are carefully developed by literacy experts and combine standards-based content with developmentally appropriate text.

Level 1 provides the most support through repetition of high-frequency words, light text, predictable sentence patterns, and strong visual support.

Level 2 offers early readers a bit more challenge through varied simple sentences, increased text load, and less repetition of high-frequency words.

Level 3 advances early-fluent readers toward fluency through increased text and concept load, less reliance on visuals, longer sentences, and more literary language.

Level 4 builds reading stamina by providing more text per page, increased use of punctuation, greater variation in sentence patterns, and increasingly challenging vocabulary.

Level 5 encourages children to move from "learning to read" to "reading to learn" by providing even more text, varied writing styles, and less familiar topics.

Whichever book is right for your reader, Blastoff! Readers are the perfect books to build confidence and encourage a love of reading that will last a lifetime!

This edition first published in 2011 by Bellwether Media, Inc.

No part of this publication may be reproduced in whole or in part without written permission of the publisher. For information regarding permission, write to Bellwether Media, Inc., Attention: Permissions Department, 5357 Penn Avenue South, Minneapolis, MN 55419.

Library of Congress Cataloging-in-Publication Data
Zobel, Derek, 1983–
  Rabbits / by Derek Zobel.
    p. cm. — (Blastoff! readers. Backyard wildlife)
  Summary: "Developed by literacy experts for students in kindergarten through grade three, this book introduces rabbits to young readers through leveled text and related photos"—Provided by publisher.
  Includes bibliographical references and index.
  ISBN 978-1-60014-443-1 (hardcover : alk. paper)
  1. Rabbits—Juvenile literature. I. Title.
QL737.L32Z63 2010
599.32—dc22   2010010683

Printed in the United States of America, North Mankato, MN.

080110   1162

Contents

Rabbits are small,
furry animals.
They hop around
on the tips of
their toes.

Rabbits have small
front legs and
large back legs.

Rabbits hit their legs against the ground to talk to other rabbits.

Rabbits often wiggle their noses. This helps them smell and breathe.

11

Rabbits live in grasslands, deserts, forests, and **wetlands**.

Rabbits eat grass, twigs, and plants. They also eat from gardens!

Rabbits have big eyes. They look for **predators** on the ground and in the sky.

Big ears help rabbits hear predators. They **freeze** when they hear danger.

Then rabbits run
away quickly.
They **zigzag**
back and forth
to escape
predators. Run!

Glossary

freeze—to suddenly stop moving

predators—animals that hunt other animals for food

wetlands—land where there is a lot of water in the ground

zigzag—to move forward while also moving from side to side; rabbits confuse predators by not running away in a straight line.

To Learn More

AT THE LIBRARY

Sexton, Colleen A. *Bunnies*. Minneapolis, Minn.: Bellwether Media, 2008.

Swanson, Diane. *Welcome to the World of Rabbits and Hares*. Milwaukee, Wisc.: Gareth Stevens Publishing, 2002.

Tagholm, Sally. *The Rabbit*. New York, N.Y.: Kingfisher, 2000.

ON THE WEB

Learning more about rabbits is as easy as 1, 2, 3.

1. Go to www.factsurfer.com.

2. Enter "rabbits" into the search box.

3. Click the "Surf" button and you will see a list of related Web sites.

With factsurfer.com, finding more information is just a click away.

Index